# THE GIRL WHO COULD FIX ANYTHING

## Beatrice Shilling, World War II Engineer

written by Mara Rockliff

illustrated by Daniel Duncan

CANDLEWICK PRESS

HARDWARE PAINT VARNISH & OILS

PEARCE'S HARDWARE

OPEN

Beatrice Shilling wasn't quite like other children.

She preferred tools to sweets.

Tools were so marvelous for making things,
and fixing things, and taking things apart!

Beatrice could make anything . . .

fix anything . . .

and when she took a thing apart,

she put it back together better than before.

One day, Beatrice and her mother went to London to meet a woman named Miss Partridge. Miss Partridge was an engineer. Her work was bringing electricity to villages, and she wanted a clever girl to help.

Beatrice was going to be an apprentice engineer!

It wasn't easy work.

Sometimes Beatrice made mistakes.

But she loved learning something new.

Miss Partridge said Beatrice should study at a university.

Beatrice wasn't quite like other students.

She was clever with her books, but even cleverer with tools.
In her spare time, she tinkered with her motorcycle.

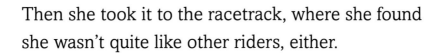

Then she took it to the racetrack, where she found
she wasn't quite like other riders, either.

She was faster.

By the time Beatrice left the university, there wasn't much she didn't know about machines. Yet no one seemed to have a job for somebody who wasn't quite like other graduates.

At last, the Royal Aircraft Establishment hired Beatrice to write handbooks about plane engines.

For Beatrice, writing about engines was a boring job. She wanted to work on real engines.

Finally, the Engine Department agreed to give her a try.

Beatrice still made mistakes sometimes.

But she was as happy as could be.

She loved her job—and she had met a man named George.

George was *quite* like Beatrice. He was an engineer. He enjoyed working on machines. George even raced motorcycles, too. He was not as fast as Beatrice, but she liked him very much indeed.

The men at work gave Beatrice a lovely wedding gift.

The next year, Britain went to war.

By now, everyone at the Royal Aircraft Establishment knew that Beatrice could fix anything. She was put in charge of a small team. They dashed around the country, showing Royal Air Force pilots how to make their planes start in the coldest weather and stop their engines from icing up.

But there was one problem nobody could solve.

Fighter pilots were like acrobats. They dove and spun and twisted, trying to shoot down the enemy without being shot down themselves.

British fighter pilots flew Hurricanes and Spitfires. Both planes had the same type of engine, and that engine had a problem. When a pilot had to dive suddenly, the plane's engine often sputtered or, for a few seconds, simply quit. This was not helpful in the middle of a fight.

The trouble seemed clear: not enough fuel was getting to the engine. It should have been easy to fix. Yet nothing seemed to work.

Day after day . . .

week after week . . .

Beatrice and her team worked late into the night.

It was a big problem for the Royal Air Force.
Many engineers were searching for a solution.
But Beatrice wasn't quite like other engineers.

She found the answer.

The problem wasn't whether enough fuel got to the engine when the pilot dove. No, the real problem came an instant later, when *too much* fuel flooded in.

Changing the engine's design could fix the problem, but that would take time and money. And time and money were exactly what the British didn't have.

Luckily, they had Beatrice.

She made a little piece of metal with a hole in it that let through just the right amount of fuel. It was easy. It was cheap. It could be put on quickly at an airfield without even taking the engine out of the plane.

When Beatrice roared up on her motorcycle with her bag of tools, pilots knew they didn't have to worry anymore.

George joined the Royal Air Force as a pilot, too.

He and Beatrice missed each other terribly.
Like other couples separated by the war,
they wrote each other letters about
what they'd do when they were
back together. Maybe they should
have a baby . . .

Of course, George and Beatrice
weren't *quite* like other couples.

Beatrice decided she would rather have a plane.

# AUTHOR'S NOTE

Beatrice Shilling (1909–1990) really did fix everything. Growing up in Hampshire and Surrey, England, she spent her pocket money on hand tools, and she was so clever with her Meccano building kit that she won a prize in a national contest set up by *Meccano Magazine.*

Frustrated that she couldn't keep up on bicycle rides with her older sisters, Beatrice started saving up for her first motorcycle when she was just ten years old. At fourteen, she had enough for a secondhand two-stroke Royal Enfield, and she quickly taught herself to take apart the engine and put it back together.

Beatrice's father couldn't see what use mechanical ability was for a girl—at least, until she wired his bedroom light so he could switch it on and off from bed instead of having to get up. But her mother recognized her talent and encouraged her.

Other women also played key roles in Beatrice's success. Dame Caroline Haslett, secretary of the Women's Engineering Society, sent a letter to girls' schools all over England advertising the electrical apprenticeship that Beatrice won. Miss Margaret Partridge and a fellow engineer, Margaret Rowbotham, gave Beatrice textbooks and urged her to apply to Victoria University of Manchester, and the London and National Society for Women's Service gave her an interest-free loan to help her pay tuition, as the engineering program offered scholarships only to men.

Despite graduating with honors in electrical engineering and going on to earn her master of science doing research on internal combustion engines, Beatrice found it hard to get a job in her field. Hearing that she placed first at Brooklands racetrack on a motorcycle she had modified herself, one interviewer said, "I suppose the men let you win."

Even after being hired by the Royal Aircraft Establishment, Beatrice faced discrimination. Sent to an airplane factory to learn about its engines, she was told that the chief engineer did not allow women inside the building, and she had to duck out of sight whenever he passed by.

Beatrice was an enthusiastic member of the Women's Engineering Society, which helped her get her start, and she encouraged other women to become engineers. She broke barriers, from defying a law against women working at night to entering the all-male "Senior Mess" (club and dining hall for higher-ups) at the Royal Aircraft Establishment. Beatrice never understood why anything should matter other than how well she did the work.

Like everyone in Britain at the time, Beatrice learned to make do with what she had on hand. Years afterward, she wrote about a fuel experiment done with only a thermos and two sides of foolscap paper for the math. She noted with pride that "the Americans" later spent $100,000 to obtain the same results.

Beatrice's marriage to George Naylor was remarkable for its equality, its happiness, and the variety of engine parts scattered around their home. It was said that Beatrice made her own wedding ring of stainless steel (not true, though she did keep a lathe in the parlor). It was also said that, having won her own Gold Star for going faster than 100 miles per hour at Brooklands racetrack in 1934, Beatrice refused to marry George until he had a Gold Star, too. Like Beatrice, George preferred airplanes to infants. The couple never ended up buying a plane, but Beatrice adored learning to fly.

After her marriage, Beatrice was still called Miss Shilling—to her face. Behind her back, some of the men she worked with called her "Tilly," after the no-frills utility trucks used in World War II. Beatrice was indeed much like a tilly: small but strong (when she tightened a nut, even George couldn't loosen it), practical, and good at getting the job done.

Particularly as she got older, those who didn't know her often underestimated her. Years after the war, the editor of *Motor Sport* magazine took Beatrice to a meeting of the British Motor Cycle Club. "Everyone ignored her," he remembered, "until we told them that she was a Gold Star 100 mph holder."

To those who did know her, Beatrice was a legend. She could tell what was wrong with an engine just by listening to it run. Even as a senior member of the Royal Aircraft Establishment, according to the *Telegraph*, "she was renowned for rolling up her sleeves and getting her hands dirty—shopworkers respected the fact that she could braze a butt joint between two pieces of copper with the skill of a fitter."

Although most famous for her achievements during World War II, especially inventing the restrictor that saved the Spitfire and the Hurricane, after the war Beatrice did pioneering work on supersonic engines, rocket fuel, and even tiny inflatable spy planes to be dropped by parachute with secret agents (sadly, these last didn't pan out). She even helped design and build a bobsled for the Royal Air Force's Olympic team.

She also worked to improve runway safety and investigated accidents. After a crash that killed twenty-three people, including eight members of the Manchester United football team, it was Beatrice who cleared the pilot's name, showing that the crash was caused by runway slush that slowed the plane on takeoff, not by the pilot failing to deice his wings.

In 1949, Beatrice was honored by King George VI with the Order of the British Empire. Twenty years later, however, she retired from the Royal Aircraft Establishment without ever reaching a top post. Such jobs were held only by men.

Beatrice had other things to think about. She had a new Jaguar—the fastest car in Britain. Still, if she took apart the engine, perhaps she could make it go just a little faster . . .

# SELECTED SOURCES

Broadbent, T. E. *Electrical Engineering at Manchester University: 125 Years of Achievement*. Manchester, UK: Manchester School of Engineering, University of Manchester, 1998.

Freudenberg, Matthew. *Negative Gravity: A Life of Beatrice Shilling*. Taunton, UK: Charlton Publications, 2003.

"Obituaries: Beatrice 'Tilly' Shilling." *The Sunday Telegraph*, November 18, 1990.

*The Woman Engineer*: The following articles, arranged by date, can be accessed via the Institution of Engineering and Technologies digital archives of the journal at www.theiet.org/publishing /library-archives/the-iet-archives.

    Partridge, Margaret M. "Lighting Problems in Country Districts." December 1923.

    "Passing Events: Miss Beatrice Shilling." December 1926.

    "News of Members." September–October 1931.

    "Research on Internal Combustion Engines." September–October 1933.

    "News of W.E.S. Members." September–October 1935.

    "News of Members." September 1936.

    "News of Members." Winter 1948–1949.

    Shilling, B. "Embarking on an Engineering Career in the Twenties." Summer 1969.

    "Women in Engineering—Past, Present and Future: Discussion." Winter 1969.

    "Miss Shilling Receives Honorary Degree from Surrey University." Spring 1970.

    "The Past: Personal Experiences Presented by Two Members." Winter 1986.

    "Beatrice Shilling." Spring 1991.

    "Miss Shilling Remembered." Autumn 2009.

Special thanks to Dr. Christine Twigg, formerly of the University of Manchester Faculty of Science and Engineering; Dr. Nina Baker, historian of the Women's Engineering Society; and Alan Brown, Geoff Butler, Brian Luff, Claire Pateman, and David Wilson of Farnborough Air Sciences Trust.

To Carter, who isn't quite like other editors—
thanks for getting Beatrice off the ground!
MR


For Nancy
DD

Text copyright © 2021 by Mara Rockliff
Illustrations copyright © 2021 by Daniel Duncan

First edition 2021

Library of Congress Catalog Card Number 2021946444
ISBN 978-1-5362-1252-5

22 23 24 25 26 CCP 10 9 8 7 6 5 4 3 2

Printed in Shenzhen, Guangdong, China

This book was typeset in Amasis Pro.
The illustrations were created digitally.

Candlewick Press
99 Dover Street
Somerville, Massachusetts 02144

www.candlewick.com